ORTHODOXY AND INNOVATION IN THE LAW OF NATIONS

BY

C. WILFRED JENKS

MACCABAEAN LECTURE IN JURISPRUDENCE
BRITISH ACADEMY
1971

FROM THE PROCEEDINGS OF THE BRITISH ACADEMY, VOLUME LVII
LONDON: OXFORD UNIVERSITY PRESS
ELY HOUSE, W. 1

Oxford University Press, Ely House, London, W. 1

GLASGOW NEW YORK TORONTO MELBOURNE WELLINGTON
CAPE TOWN IBADAN NAIROBI DAR ES SALAAM LUSAKA ADDIS ABABA
DELHI BOMBAY CALCUTTA MADRAS KARACHI LAHORE DACCA
KUALA LUMPUR SINGAPORE HONG KONG TOKYO

ISBN 0 19 725668 6

PRINTED IN GREAT BRITAIN

MACCABAEAN LECTURE IN JURISPRUDENCE

ORTHODOXY AND INNOVATION IN THE LAW OF NATIONS

By C. WILFRED JENKS

Read 12 May 1971

WE no longer live in the world into which we were born. The world has changed more in our lifetimes than during any comparable period of previous history. In some respects it has changed more in our lifetimes than throughout previously recorded history. The rhythm of change is still gaining acceleration. Technology, economics, social habit, cultural values, politics, morals, indeed every aspect of life in society, all are in flux. Stability has now become the exception to change rather than change the exception to stability. This much we all concede, however reluctantly.

What has this done to the law, to the place of law in society, and to the concept of law itself? For many of us law has always been primarily a factor of stability in society; for others its role as a factor of orderly change has been hardly less important. In the contemporary cataclysm of constant and cumulative change what continuing cogency has Maitland's warning that 'the lawyer must be orthodox otherwise he is no lawyer'?[1] What degree of shift of emphasis to Roscoe Pound's insistence on reconciling 'the need of stability with the inevitableness of change' has now become appropriate and perhaps indispensable?[2] How inhibiting is the obligation of orthodoxy? What measure of innovation can we reconcile with orthodoxy? In what measure has innovation now become orthodox? What is now the accepted orthodoxy of innovation? What of the fear that boldness in innovation may substitute 'subjective' standards for 'objective' orthodoxy? These are large questions of policy. They arise with a peculiar acuteness because neither the future of law in society nor the willingness of society to continue to

[1] *Collected Papers* (Cambridge University Press, 1911), vol. i, p. 49.

[2] *The Formative Era of American Law* (Boston, Little, Brown, and Co., 1938), p. 13.

respect the rule of law can be taken for granted. They have become the central dilemma of all the leading legal systems. In international law they are still more vital. Our response to these questions will fulfil or destroy the prospect of creating an organized world community instinct with the rule of law.

There is no lack of awareness of the issue in the highest counsels of the law. It has been stated with particular clarity and cogency in the extra-judicial pronouncements of some of the highest judicial authorities. Thus Chief Justice Warren, addressing the American Bar Association in Westminster Hall, has told us that the common law has been received in the United States 'in its most significant and vital aspect, not as a fixed body of rules, but as a mode of ascertaining and devising rules to meet the particular circumstances and changing conditions in which controversies and conflicts arise between man and man and man and government'.[1] It is, he says, a fact and not a boast that 'in all the countries where English is the tongue of the law, the common law has shown itself to be a process of constant rejuvenation to meet the demands of a progressive society'. Chief Justice Gajendragadkar of India, in his Lala Lajpat Rai Memorial Lectures, has expressed essentially the same philosophy. 'Law in relation to liberty and social justice has to be considered', he says, 'in its aspect of a flexible instrument of social change and social adjustment. . . . It is a social institution, democratically evolved in order to achieve the object of making social adjustments to meet the challenge which necessarily and incessantly flows from unsatisfied, legitimate human desires and ambitions.'[2] Chief Justice Sir Adetokunbo Ademola of Nigeria has spoken in much the same terms. 'No system of law', he says, 'is self-sustaining, even as today no country by itself can stand alone. You cannot stand today as a mere observer; the law must move as fast as the world moves. . . . Our law and our society must not be hampered by the inflexibility of the Common Law; they must grow to meet the challenges of the changing world.'[3]

How relevant is this approach to the present predicament of the law of nations, the unprecedented pressure of the challenge

[1] *The Public Papers of Chief Justice Earl Warren* (New York, Simon and Schuster, 1959), p. 104.

[2] P. B. Gajendragadkar, *Law, Liberty and Social Justice* (Bombay, Asia Publishing House, 1965), p. 45.

[3] Address to the General Conference of the Nigeria Bar Association, 26 March 1959.

to the law to keep pace with life? What bearing has it on the future prospects of international adjudication, at present so precariously uncertain? How consistent is it with the present temper of the common law in 'its old home'[1] where judicial innovation remains within narrower limits than in some of the newer jurisdictions? How far is the measure of judicial innovation accepted by the present temper of the common law in 'its old home' adequate to ensure the relevance and effectiveness of judicial process in the present stage of development of international society?

It has been powerfully argued that the great judge, the judge who 'was great because when the occasion cried out for new law he dared to make it',[2] has become obsolete in England. If this be true it involves the abdication of a great tradition. Law 'is made by men',[3] and in the light of the history of the common law 'English lawyers, of all men, should believe in the power of the great judge'.[3] Among those who hold that judicial innovation has ceased to be a significant influence on the growth of English law is Lord Devlin, who has said: 'The work done by the Judges of England is not now as glorious as it was. The opportunities are not what they used to be nor are they the equal of those which judges have seized in other countries administering the common law. There are no great constitutional questions for English judges to decide. . . . They have no such exciting tasks as . . . that of fusing English law with indigenous law.'[4] There are many such exciting tasks in the international arena, indeed more of them than ever before. Lord Devlin gives a twofold explanation for the receding rather than expanding influence in England not of the judiciary alone but of the common law itself. The nature of the process of developing law by precedent inevitably implies that the multiplication of precedents progressively limits the scope for further developments. The increasing importance of legislation, while further narrowing the scope for judicial innovation, makes such innovation less necessary as the opportunity for it becomes more limited.[5]

1 The expression comes from Lord Wright, speaking at Harvard, *Legal Essays and Addresses* (Cambridge University Press, 1939), p. 72.

2 Louis L. Jaffe, *English and American Judges as Lawmakers* (Oxford, Clarendon Press, 1969), p. 13.

3 C. H. S. Fifoot, *Judge and Jurist in the Reign of Victoria* (London, Stevens, 1959), p. 12.

4 *Samples of Law Making* (Oxford University Press, 1962), p. 6.

5 Ibid., pp. 115–16.

Neither of these factors is operative in the same manner or degree in the present stage of development of international law and international adjudication. One may even hope that their present importance is a phase of arrested development rather than the final chapter in the development of the common law in England. It would be tragic if habits of thought moulded by them were to inhibit the vitality of the British contribution to the future of international adjudication. Any such tendency would be inconsistent with the tradition which the expansion of the common law has made familiar to a wider world. It would indeed be a denial of the traditional British approach to international law itself. The British approach to international law, as we inherited it from Phillimore and Hall, Westlake and Lorimer, and as it has been developed in the twentieth century by Brierly and Fischer Williams, McNair and Lauterpacht, has always found expression in the formulation of living principles rather than a positivist insistence on strict proof of the consent of States to particular formulations of specific rules.

It has been suggested that there is now a fundamental divergence between a view accepted by the majority of British international lawyers that international law is a set of neutral rules which it is the task of the judge to apply objectively to the facts before him, and a view now accepted by the majority of American international lawyers that international law is a decision-making process in which the judge must exercise policy-making options by weighing the conflicting interests of the parties in the context of the interests of the world community as a whole.[1] I am, I gather, alleged to lean towards the American rather than the British view, though with appropriately British restraint. Without wholly rejecting this allegation, I am not persuaded of the presumed antithesis on which it is based. For my part I regard the articulation of such a fundamental divergence as being as premature as a matter of legal analysis as it is undesirable as a matter of high policy. Expressed as absolutes these are of course conflicting philosophies, but neither represents a fixed national attitude irreconcilable with the other. There have been, within our lifetimes, and may well be again, periods in which British jurisprudence has been much bolder and American jurisprudence much more cautious, and there are some current signs of a changing emphasis on both sides of

[1] Rosalyn Higgins, 'Policy Considerations and the International Judicial Process', *The International and Comparative Law Quarterly*, 4th Series, vol. 17, part I, January 1968, pp. 58–84.

the Atlantic. If we concede that a schism has occurred between contemporary British and American legal thinking on the range of judicial innovation, the schism has not been inevitable;[1] it should not be assumed to be perpetual or even necessarily of long duration, and must not be allowed to crystallize into contrasted attitudes to the future of international adjudication.

The case for judicial caution in international courts and tribunals, which it is as unwise to despise as to overstate, rests primarily on grounds which neither reflect nor presuppose any such assumed divergence of contemporary national attitudes towards judicial innovation. Thus, Sir Gerald Fitzmaurice, who has emphasized that the uses of judicial innovation are offset by its perils and that 'a judicial innovation (indeed *especially* a judicial one), however desirable it might be from other standpoints, is too dearly purchased if it is made at the sacrifice of the integrity of the law', fully concedes that neither the common law of England nor the civil law of ancient Rome would ever have come into being without judicial innovation, and that 'modern experience shows that even in fully developed legal systems' such innovation remains necessary 'and goes on all the time' because it is 'beyond the normal capacity of any legislature to provide in advance for all the subtilties, the twists, the turns and the by-ways resulting from novel and constantly changing conditions' or to 'anticipate great issues of principle which may arrive suddenly, and indeed for the first time, through the medium of a litigation.'[2] How much more true is this in the present stage of development of international law, in which the 'steady pressure of human developments'[3] upon the law is so insistent and the law-making capacity of the treaty-making process and other international legislative procedures is so limited. The crucial point is that 'since specific legislative action with direct binding effect is not at present possible in the international legal field, judicial pronouncements of one kind or another constitute the principal method by which the law can find some concrete measure of clarification and development'.[4] Judges considering that the International Court has

[1] Ibid., p. 84.

[2] 'Judicial Innovation—Its Uses and its Perils', in *Cambridge Essays in International Law in Honour of Lord McNair* (London, Stevens, 1965), pp. 24–47.

[3] Sir John Fischer Williams, *Chapters on Current International Law and the League of Nations* (London, Longmans, 1929), p. 477.

[4] Separate Opinion of Sir Gerald Fitzmaurice in *Barcelona Traction Case*, 1970, I.C.J., 65.

rested its decision on too narrow a basis have frequently invoked this as a justification for a wider exposition of their views in a separate or dissenting opinion, but the point has a broader and deeper thrust.

Integrity is fundamental, but integrity, as distinguished from coherence and consistency, is a concept applicable to the processes rather than the content of the law. Coherence and consistency, important as they are for the intelligibility of the law, for its credibility and credit as the expression of justice, and for convenience in its administration, are not absolute values. They can never be wholly reconciled with the inevitability of growth and change, and are therefore always blurred with margins of uncertainty which widen in times of dramatic growth and change. Integrity must be measured by higher standards than coherence and consistency alone where these fall short of justice. We must seek it in the persistent quest for justice in a changing and ever more complex world, rather than in a static situation. This is to state the problem rather than to solve it. Interwoven with the question of integrity but by no means identical with it is that of confidence. Judicial innovation tends to strain the confidence of those who dislike the innovation; judicial caution tends to forfeit the confidence of those who regard the law as imprisoning them in the past. This is a difficult dilemma for any legal system, especially dangerous where jurisdiction is voluntary, as that of international courts and tribunals so largely remains. Where jurisdiction is compulsory, confidence is primarily a question of respect for decisions and ease of enforcement. Where jurisdiction is voluntary, no confidence means no jurisdiction, and, failing a common professionalism which commands general respect, the confidence of conflicting parties may presuppose irreconcilable anticipations of the result. These are fundamental issues. The integrity of the legal process and confidence of the community (though not, alas, always of the parties) in the result are the warp and woof of the law; without them, closely knit, it loses all texture. How are we to avoid any sacrifice of integrity without surrender to immobility (the perils of which, though perhaps less apparent, are no less grave than those of reckless innovation) and to broaden confidence in the law despite the clash of conflicting interests involved in the continuing tension between stability and change?

The range of questions in respect of which these issues may be acute covers all the vital areas in which the law is in movement: the control of force; the erosion of sovereignty by common interests, and by habits, procedures, and obligations of mutual consultation and collective action; the regulation of armament; the peaceful settlement of disputes; the general welfare as a legal interest; the collective stake in human rights and in particular in civil liberties; the legal framework of economic stability and growth; the social discipline of science and technology; the contribution of international organizations to the law; the place therein of multinational entities of the most varied types; the institutional structure of an organized world community; the development in such a community of more effective legislative, judicial, and administrative processes; the status of its agents; the finances of the community; and the sources from which the law recruits new principles and rules in all these areas.

In respect of all these matters we are clearly passing through a period of fundamental change the outcome of which will determine whether we succeed in integrating or irrevocably disrupt the framework of an orderly world society.

Difficult as the problems are there is much that is encouraging. We must not underestimate the changes made in the law by legislative action during the last half-century despite the deficiencies of international legislative procedure and limitations of international legislative action. Most fundamental has been the change in the legal status of war and legality of force effected by the General Treaty for the Renunciation of War and the Charter of the United Nations. Human rights, comprehensively defined by the Universal Declaration of Human Rights and by the United Nations Covenants which are not yet in force, are now the subject of a comprehensive network of international and regional agreements[1] in varying stages of ratification and of varied degrees of effectiveness. Monetary policy and trade are governed by the Articles of Agreement of the International Monetary Fund and the GATT Agreements and aviation and telecommunications by ICAO and ITU regulations. The Antarctic Treaty, the Nuclear Test Ban Treaty, and the Space Treaty are perhaps only the opening gambit of a whole series of agreements providing an agreed legal framework for scientific and technological developments. And these are but examples of a trend which embraces the international facet of every aspect of contemporary life. In all these matters bold innovations have superseded old orthodoxies.

[1] Cf. Ian Brownlie, *Basic Documents on Human Rights* (Oxford, Clarendon Press, 1971).

Neither must we underestimate the impact on the law of the institutional development of the last half-century. The concept of sovereignty may be constantly reiterated from old and new quarters alike, but its reality and relevance are being constantly eroded by the increasingly effective expression in institutional arrangements and institutionalized procedures of common interests and collective responsibilities. Human rights, monetary policy, and trade are three outstanding examples of matters regarded half a century ago as solely within the domestic jurisdiction of each state which are now subject to continuing international consultation and review. Developments of this nature have been made possible by, and are increasingly reflected in, legal devices, procedures, and techniques which are startling innovations when compared with orthodox practice.

Nor must we underestimate the effect of the process of codifying international law which is gradually becoming a reality. During the inter-war period the progress of codification came to a dead stop and when the United Nations resumed the task there was widespread scepticism. Despite the increasing difficulty of the task in an increasingly difficult world the outlook is now far more encouraging. The United Nations Conferences on the Law of the Sea, on Diplomatic and Consular Immunities, and on the Law of Treaties, have made, on the basis of the work of the International Law Commission, substantial progress and, though uncertainties remain concerning the extent to which the conventions adopted will be ratified and the future work of the Commission itself, the process of codification may already have played a decisive part in effecting the transition from a public law of the Western World which the Second and Third Worlds were apt to reject to a freely accepted common law of mankind, still in gestation but clearly coming to birth. This has been done by a subtle tempering of orthodoxy by innovation and of innovation by orthodoxy.

It follows from all of this that the legal framework within which international adjudication now operates has changed as dramatically as its political context. A substantial element of innovation in the outcome of international adjudication is the inevitable and direct result of changes in the law which are not themselves attributable to judicial innovation. Even for those who circumscribe their judicial duty by the law as they find it, the law as they find it is one in which orthodoxy has been heavily dosed with innovation. How far should the judicial art itself add a further ingredient of innovation? Clearly it must give full faith and credit to the innovations effected in these other ways and not hesitate to deduce their implications and apply them in full. How much further should it go by judicial innovation which goes beyond the limitations of judicial recognition of the full consequences of other innovations? How do we keep the balance true between orthodoxy which spells stagnation and innovation which approaches irresponsibility? How do we avoid the erosion of confidence on either score?

Here we touch the kernel of the matter. Much of contemporary scholarship is alert to the tempo of change. An important vein of current statesmanship is conscious of the challenge. The plea that the creative imagination must be a major catalyst in reshaping the law by drawing new implications and applications from recognized general principles, by upholding the continuing vitality of custom, by vigorous legislative action, and by purposive institution building,[1] has been widely heard. What bearing has this innovative temper of the contemporary legal mind on the established orthodoxy of international adjudication? How far has adjudication a correlative responsibility to move with the times? How consistent is such a responsibility with its essential nature as adjudication? How sensitive is international adjudication to the measure in which it has such a responsibility? Is it ungenerous to inquire whether there may not on occasion be, in assessing the measure of this responsibility, a generation gap between the architects and craftsmen who are determined to rebuild the law and those who determine it judicially in international courts and tribunals? What part can the British contribution to the international judicial temper play in the coming years in fulfilling the historic role of the common law by enlisting empirical boldness in a commonsense response to human need?

I have been over-general for over-long and you may reasonably be impatient that I should test these generalities by the specifics of specific cases. What progress, if any, are we making in reconciling orthodoxy and innovation in an acceptable pattern of international adjudication which represents a positive contribution to the progress of law in world affairs? And if our progress report should be discouraging, what can the temper of British jurisprudence contribute to a more hopeful and positive solution of the dilemmas which confront us?

In all three of the most recent decisions of the International

[1] As I have made it in, for instance, *A New World of Law?* (London, Longmans, 1969).

Court of Justice, the *South West Africa Cases*,[1] the *North Sea Continental Shelf Cases*,[2] and the *Case Concerning the Barcelona Traction, Light and Power Company Ltd.*,[3] some of these issues have been brought into sharp relief and they may well emerge equally sharply in the *Namibia Case* now pending before the Court. Taken together, these cases cover three of the areas in which the law is most clearly in movement: human rights as a matter of concern to the whole civilized world; the interplay of technological development and the growth of custom; and the increasing complexity of international corporate structures. How far do these decisions augur well for, or create anxiety concerning, the future effectiveness of the rule of law in world affairs and what kind of challenge do they represent for the future contribution of British jurisprudence to international adjudication?

The judgments and opinions in these cases run to some 1,100 pages and the published pleadings, not yet complete, already amount to some 20 substantial volumes; any detailed analysis of them is therefore impracticable and I must be content to comment on some salient points.

The *South West Africa Cases* have attracted much and heated attention.

Ethiopia and Liberia, as former Members of the League of Nations, claimed essentially that the practice of *apartheid* was a violation of the League of Nations mandate for South West Africa which was still binding upon South Africa.[4] The Court on 18 July 1966, by the casting vote of the President, the votes being equally divided, rejected the claims of Ethiopia and Liberia on the ground that they had not 'established any legal right or interest appertaining to them in the subject matter of the claim'.[5] The emotional tension of this result, attributable primarily to the issues at stake, was accentuated by an accumulation of factors which deepened a widespread sense of unfairness: the dismissal of the case on the ground that the parties had no standing after five years of intensive consideration and four years after the Court had upheld its jurisdiction to adjudicate upon the merits of the dispute; the sharp division of opinion within the Court; the decisive effect on the voting of the absence of three judges all of whom it was believed would have upheld the claims, one of these absences being due to death, the second to sickness, and the third to the judge's being held to be disqualified by the President who was subsequently

[1] 1966, I.C.J., 3–505. [2] 1969, I.C.J., 4–257. [3] 1970, I.C.J., 4–357.
[4] *South West Africa Cases*, 1966, I.C.J., 6–505. [5] Ibid., p. 51.

to give the casting vote in opposition to the presumed view of the disqualified judge; the resting of the decision on a theory that the applicants had no legal right or interest which had not even been advanced by the respondent in its final submissions, still less fully argued. One can hardly conceive of a more unfortunate combination of strains upon credibility and confidence in a situation in which the known emotional climate of the issue, involving pent-up racial tension throughout the world, called for an exceptional serenity of treatment. In these circumstances it is not surprising that the decision, and the alignment of judges for and against, should have been widely regarded as a capitulation of the supreme judicial organ of the United Nations to political influences. There was at the time sharp dissent from this view. Thus it was said that 'in five or six years' it will 'be realized that this Case was a great turning point' because the Court 'did not give way to political pressure' but showed that it was 'not to be browbeaten by political considerations'.[1] There is no indication that this prediction is likely to be fulfilled even over a much longer period. On the contrary the last five years have crystallized general acceptance of the view that, whatever one may think of the issues involved, the practical outcome of the proceedings was in every respect disastrous. The rejection of the claim on the ground that the applicants had no standing was questionable in law, and practically unwise for substantially the reasons for which Lord Denning, two days ago, declined to base on no standing his rejection of Mr. Blackburn's claim that the Crown is not entitled to sign the Treaty of Rome.[2]

It is, however, profoundly unfair to the Court and its members, and a grave disservice to the future of international adjudication, to regard the division of view which attracted attention in so dramatic a manner as being exclusively or even primarily due to political considerations or influences. The crux of the case was a choice between conflicting legal philosophies in a context highly charged with emotional tension and circumstances calculated to maximize suspicion of motive and distrust of integrity. The fundamentals of the issue—and they are the central issue of all judicial responsibility—can be reduced from the five hundred pages of the judgment and opinions to a few broad propositions. The seven judges who became the majority by the casting vote of the President took the view that the duty of the International Court is 'to apply the law as it finds it, not

[1] Sir Francis Vallat in *The Times*, 31 October 1966, p. 9.

[2] *Blackburn* v. *Attorney General*, *The Times*, 11 May 1971, p. 10.

to make it'.[1] The seven judges who remained the minority dissented on grounds which one of them, Judge Tanaka, expressed as being that the historical development of law is a 'continual process of the cultural enrichment of the legal order by taking account values or interests which had previously been excluded from the sphere of law'.[2] For the majority the Court

> is a court of law and can take account of moral principles only in so far as these are given a sufficient expression in legal form. Law exists, it is said, to serve a social need; but precisely for that reason it can do so only through and within the limits of its own discipline. Otherwise, it is not a legal service that would be rendered. Humanitarian considerations may constitute the inspirational basis for rules of law. . . . Such considerations do not, however, in themselves amount to rules of law. All states are interested—have an interest—in such matters. But the existence of an interest does not of itself entail that this interest is specifically juridical in character. . . . In order to generate legal rights and obligations, it must be given juridical expression and clothed in legal form.

For the minority, again speaking through Judge Tanaka, a court of law does not legislate but,

> where the borderline can be drawn is a very delicate and difficult matter. Of course, judges declare the law, but they do not function automatically. We cannot deny the possibility of some degree of creative element in their judicial activities. What is not permitted to judges is to establish the law independently of an existing legal system, institution or norm. What is permitted to them is to declare what can be logically inferred from the *raison d'être* of a legal system, institution or norm. In the latter case the lacuna in the intent of legislation or parties can be filled.[3]

It is in the course of this process, one might continue, that moral principles are given 'a sufficient expression in legal form', that the law draws 'the limits of its own discipline', and that interests become 'specifically juridical in character'.

These are clearly fundamental questions the answers to which will determine the extent to which law remains the accepted discipline of a changing society, is rejected as irrelevant to the pressures of change, or becomes so much the creature of those pressures that it ceases to guide and discipline them. If we seek to solve grave problems by dialogue rather than by violence, and to preserve due process of law as a possible option for those who challenge the *status quo* (now comprising the great majority

[1] 1966, I.C.J., 48. [2] 1966, I.C.J., 252. [3] 1966 I.C.J., 277.

of mankind), we must provide within the law for the inevitability of change. Has the spirit of the common law, as nurtured in its 'old home', still the reserves of moral and intellectual vitality necessary to resolve the dilemma in a manner acceptable to the whole world? For my part I do not think so ill of the law, or of British jurisprudence, as to be willing to tolerate a negative answer.

In the *North Sea Continental Shelf Cases*[1] and *Barcelona Traction Case*[2] we find the Court wrestling with problems which were more manageable, in that they did not have the same highly explosive emotional content, but raised no less acutely the question of the part of judicial process in processes of growth and change in the law.

The *North Sea Continental Shelf Cases*,[3] judgment in which was given on 20 February 1969, related to the competing claims of the Federal Republic of Germany, Denmark, and the Netherlands to certain areas of continental shelf in the North Sea. The case reflects the increasing exploitation of oil and gas deposits in the sea-bed of the North Sea. The role entrusted to the Court was not that of settling the dispute but that of determining the principles and rules of international law applicable to the delimitation of the contested areas by agreements between the parties. The Court found, by eleven votes to six, that the use of the equidistance method of delimitation was not obligatory as between the parties; that the delimitation of the contested areas was to be effected by agreement in such a way as to leave as much as possible to each party all those parts of the continental shelf that constituted a natural prolongation of its land territory into and under the sea, without encroachment on the natural prolongation of the land territory of the other; and that if such delimitation left to the parties areas that overlapped, these were to be divided between them in agreed proportions or, failing agreement, equally, unless they decided on a regime of joint jurisdiction, use, or exploitation for the zones of overlap or any part of them. Three factors were to be taken into account in the negotiations: the general configuration of the coasts and any unusual features; so far as known or readily ascertainable, the physical and geological structure, and natural resources, of the areas involved; and the element of a reasonable degree of proportionality between the extent of the continental shelf areas appertaining to the coastal state and the length of its coast.

[1] 1969, I.C.J., 3–257.
[2] 1970, I.C.J., 3–357.
[3] 1969, I.C.J., 3–257.

At first glance these may appear to be technicalities, with little or no bearing on the larger issues which will determine the responsiveness of the law to contemporary need, but when we pass from the findings of the judgment to the reasoning of the opinions we find ourselves wrestling with much bigger issues than the application of the principle of equidistance in the delimitation of the continental shelf. They include such questions as whether the law recognizes claims to a 'just and equitable share' of the continental shelf to be determined by a process of apportionment rather than delimitation (which involves the larger question of the relationship between 'just and equitable shares' and established legal rights in other matters), the circumstances in which a conventional regime becomes binding on states not parties thereto, the rate of formation of custom in contemporary society, the relationship between rules which operate automatically and principles the application of which involves a discretionary element, and the factual elements in the balancing of equities within the limits of the application of legal principles. These are significant elements in the capacity of the law to keep pace with life in a world of change. The division of view in the Court on these fundamental matters did not wholly coincide with the voting on the specific findings on which the Court based its decision.

On some major points there was a measure of agreement which is both encouraging and sobering, encouraging as a demonstration that at a time of so much instability and disagreement not everything is at large, sobering as a reminder that any recasting of the fundamentals of the law lies beyond the maximum range of potential judicial innovation.

The Court was unanimous in rejecting any suggestion that claims to the continental shelf can be determined by the apportionment of 'just and equitable' shares. It did so on the ground that the notion 'of apportioning an as yet undetermined area' is 'quite foreign to and inconsistent with, the basic concept of continental shelf entitlement, according to which the process of delimitation is essentially one of drawing a boundary line between areas which already appertain to one or other of the States affected'.[1] 'Delimitation was not a matter of sharing out, among two or more states, of something common to those states.'[2]

The Court could not substitute equitable shares for legal rights, but recognized quite clearly that legal rights in a law in

[1] 1969, I.C.J., 22. [2] Ibid., Judge Morelli at p. 199.

motion are in process of being remoulded by the movement in the law. By the standards of a generation ago it is little less than a revolution that the Court should say that 'the passage of only a short period of time is not necessarily, or of itself, a bar to the formation of a new rule of customary international law'[1] and that, in the process whereby new custom becomes law, the law-making treaty may play a decisive part by serving as 'the nucleus around which a new set of generally recognised legal rules may crystallize';[2] in the language of the judgment this is 'one of the recognized methods by which new rules of customary international law may be formed'.[3]

The disputed ground was, not unnaturally, the middle ground, the issue being whether the equidistance principle as embodied in Article 6 of the 1958 Geneva Continental Shelf Convention had attained the status of customary law. This was a matter of factual appreciation rather than principle. Some have found the judgment indecisive, but what is least decisive is what is least important, its relationship to the facts of the particular case. There is no indecisiveness in the attitude of the Court to the two fundamental questions involved, that a proper respect for equities does not justify substituting equitable shares for legal rights and that the weight of alleged custom is to be measured by the rhythm of contemporary life rather than by what is shown to have been established from time immemorial. Nor did the Court hesitate to express its judgment in an innovative and potentially fruitful form resembling a decree in equity as a statement of factors to be taken into account in subsequent negotiations rather than a final determination; this was not indecision but a deliberate response to the express wish of the parties which may prove a most useful precedent for the future adaptability of international judicial procedures.

The *Continental Shelf Cases* emphasize that the dilemma which the *South West Africa Cases* appeared to pose so starkly is by no means absolute. The progress of the law is often a matter of groping. Anything comparable to the wholly new legal status for space or the ocean depths which we have achieved by other approaches lies beyond the range of judicial innovation, but within more modest limits the law is far from frozen.

How effectively are the margins of possible development being exploited to meet new needs, and how vigilant is the spirit of the common law in expanding the rule of law to embrace new

[1] Ibid., p. 43.
[2] Ibid., Judge Sorensen at p. 244.
[3] Ibid., p. 41.

territory? Some further large queries in the matter are raised by the *Barcelona Traction Case*[1] which impinged upon, without coming to grips with, the problem of the place of multinational corporations in the law of nations. In this case the Belgian Government claimed damages for losses alleged to have been suffered by Belgian shareholders of a Canadian company operating in Spain. The Court, by a judgment given on 5 February 1970 after proceedings lasting eight years in which thirty-six counsel participated, rejected the claim by fifteen votes to one, essentially on the ground, concurred in by twelve judges, that the Belgian Government had not established any *jus standi*. Nowhere in the judgment, or in the eleven opinions and declarations appended thereto, are we given an agreed or coherent picture of the real interests involved, but *Barcelona Traction* was clearly a complex corporate structure with at least some of the features of what is commonly known as a multinational corporation, heading fourteen other companies of which it had from one hundred per cent to ninety per cent control and itself controlled by another company as part of a group involving special relationships with over eighty closely linked companies.[2] In the complex there were three different nationalities of registration, irrespective of questions concerning the reality of control and the real ownership of stock.

Many will share the disappointment expressed by President Bustamante in his Separate Opinion that 'investigation reveals an almost total absence of specific rules of general international law or treaty law applicable to transnational holding companies' and that 'neither the legal systems of States nor the law-making organs of the international community have yet succeeded in grasping this elusive reality of holding companies so as to bring it within the framework of a sufficiently explicit and precise body of law'; they will agree with him that the absence of any basis on which the Court can assume jurisdiction 'does not absolve the international judge of his obligation to lay stress on the objective position of the question of principle, i.e. the existing disparity between the development of certain phenomena in international economics, such as the grouping of limited companies under what are known as holding companies, and the evolution of the law applicable' but leaves him with the duty to insist that 'the legal lacunae which have in consequence made their appearance may hamper the proper working of justice'.

1 *Case Concerning the Barcelona Traction, Light and Power Co. Ltd.*, 1970, I.C.J., 3–357.

2 Ibid., Judge Gros at p. 268.

But is it sufficient to describe this situation as 'an unsatisfactory state of the law'[1] or to say, as the Court does, that 'it may at first sight appear surprising that the evolution of law has not gone further and that no generally accepted rules in the matter have crystallized on the international plane', but that 'a more thorough examination of the facts shows that the law on the subject has been formed in a period characterized by an intense conflict of systems and interests' and that 'here as elsewhere a body of rules could only have been developed with the consent of those concerned'?[2]

The ground of the decision, that the Belgian Government had not established any *jus standi*, suggests a superficial resemblance to the *South West Africa Cases*, but the Court was at some pains to distinguish the cases. It drew 'an essential distinction' between 'the obligations of a state towards the international community as a whole and those arising *vis-à-vis* another state in the field of diplomatic protection'. The former, 'by their very nature', are 'obligations *erga omnes*'; they include obligations concerning 'the basic rights of the human person, including protection from slavery and racial discrimination'. Obligations 'the performance of which is the subject of diplomatic protection' are 'not of the same category'. There is no general legal interest in the observance of such legal obligations and to bring a claim in respect of the breach of such an obligation a state must establish its special interest. The distinction is by no means indefensible, but the outcome is nevertheless paradoxical. There may well be a more general interest in the protection of fundamental human rights than in that of claims subject to diplomatic protection. Certainly it is reassuring that the Court has in effect disavowed its decision in the *South West Africa Cases* that the applicants in that case had no standing. But has it not, from a different standpoint, been almost equally insensitive to present and future need in reaffirming the doctrine of no standing in this different context, less charged with emotional dynamite but involving some of the most fluid and dynamic elements in international economic life? Why is there so much reluctance, in respect of so varied a range of questions, to come to grips with the substantive issues?

The judgment makes a gesture to the pressure of life upon the law. 'In seeking to determine the law applicable', the Court says, it 'has to bear in mind the continuous evolution of

[1] Ibid., Sir Gerald Fitzmaurice at p. 64.

[2] Ibid., pp. 46–7.

international law'.[1] The 'profound transformations which have taken place in the economic life of nations must therefore be taken into account' and 'international law is called upon to recognize institutions of municipal law that have an important and extensive role in the international field'. But the gesture fails to come to life. The Court starts from the principle that 'whenever legal issues arise concerning the rights of states with regard to the treatment of companies and shareholders, as to which rights international law has not established its own rules, it has to refer to the relevant rules of municipal law' and deduces from this that in view of the relevance to the case of the rights of the corporate entity and its shareholders under municipal law it must devote attention to the nature and interrelation of these rights. Thus far there can be no dissent. International legal transactions are so complex in nature that international tribunals must constantly have recourse to municipal law to determine the rights and obligations which they are called upon to assess, but the spirit in which they do so may vitally affect the result. It is true, as the Court says, that in referring to 'rules generally accepted by municipal legal systems' the Court 'cannot modify, still less deform, them', but it also has an obligation to avoid petrifying them by eliminating from its consideration elements of growth and change, and equitable exceptions to rigid rules, which are essential elements of vigorous legal systems. The Court concedes that 'the law has recognized that the independent existence of the legal entity cannot be treated as an absolute'[2] but finds none of the recognized grounds for lifting the corporate veil applicable to the case. A comparison with the judgment of the separate opinions of Judges Sir Gerald Fitzmaurice, Tanaka, Jessup, and Gros suggests that the Court may have seriously underestimated the wind of change in the more vigorous legal systems in matters relating to rights within corporate entities. The outcome is anomalies which, in municipal legal systems, would certainly result in remedial legislative action; this failure to take account of 'principles directed to enabling the shareholders to act in certain kinds of cases where the action of the company is unavailable or not forthcoming, or to influence or change the management or its policy' produces 'the inadmissible consequence that important interests may go wholly unprotected, and that what may possibly be grave wrongs will, as a result, not be susceptible even of investigation'.[3] This is salutary

[1] *Case Concerning the Barcelona* . . . p. 33.
[2] Ibid., p. 39.
[3] Ibid., Sir Gerald Fitzmaurice at p. 84.

doctrine, but must we not go beyond this and express the virility of the common-law approach to international law in a remedy rather than a protest? Are we being held back by real practical difficulties or unreal conceptual limitations?

In the *Barcelona Traction Case*, as in the *North Sea Continental Shelf Cases*, the reasoning of the judgment and opinions raises far larger questions than the operative provisions of the judgment. One turns away from the case with a sense of its having been an immense irrelevancy to the real issues. It reinforces the argument for a searching reappraisal of the future contribution of the spirit of the common law to the 'constant rejuvenation' of the law and of the extent to which the common law 'in its old home' is still faithful to its pristine spirit.

We are passing through a fundamental crisis in the process of creation of an organized world community. The outcome of the crisis will determine the whole direction of the future of mankind. What part can the law play in determining the outcome of the crisis and how will the outcome of the crisis affect the future of the law? What bearing has the law as it is and might be on the prospects of an organized common peace, political stability, personal freedom, economic growth, social justice, and the impact on society of scientific and technological development? Are the limits of the law, as we might reasonably hope to develop it, at best so narrow that we must leave the larger questions to be settled by other forces? If the moral and legal values embodied in the common law do not set the tone of vigorous development, if we allow them to be identified by world opinion with the past, the future will be shaped by forces alien to the spirit of the common law. We must choose between the vigorous development of the law in the tradition of the greatest common-law judges and abdicating all influence upon its development. If we are inhibited by the rule book from grappling boldly with new problems we will leave a vacuum into which influences much less congenial to the genius of the common law will be prompt to expand. Is this in the interest of international adjudication? Is it in the interest of the rule of law? Is it in the interest of justice? Do not overriding reasons of policy and humanity exact a larger view than the conventional orthodoxies?

Such are the range and level of the issues which are at stake. Substantially more is involved than the function and influence of law in international relationships as such, vital as these are. The place of law in the national life of many countries, the nature of the law which prevails there, and the part which it plays in giving substantive and procedural reality to new ideals of freedom and providing an orderly discipline for the relentlessness of change may well depend upon the outcome. In the vast areas of the world in which the whole concept of the rule of law has hardly got beyond paper, what happens internationally and what happens nationally may affect each other decisively; how much can be achieved internationally may be determined by the trend of what is happening nationally and what in fact happens internationally may set the pattern for what can be achieved nationally, with an interplay of forces so complex that one can form no clear picture of what or how much is cause and what or how much effect. Such an appraisal of the situation does not provide, and indeed rather precludes, precise answers to particular questions, but it does afford a general standard of judgment which may be considerably more important than the precise answers to particular questions, a sense of the order of magnitude of the issues which reinvigorates fundamental principles, and a freshness of approach which declines to be dismayed by the doubts and difficulties which so often inhibit a resolute solution of unprecedented problems.

These are perhaps imponderables, but they are imponderables of such weight that we must weigh them with great deliberation against the convenience of certainty and the alleged danger of eroding integrity by innovation. The question at once arises what we mean by integrity as applied to legal principles and processes and whether the integrity which we seek to protect is the integrity of the law as such or that of rights created or recognized by the law at one stage of its development but subject to modification by due process of law as the law changes or develops. If we fail to find in the main stream of existing law, and as a logical progression from it, bold fresh answers to new questions, the integrity of the law as such, and the authority of the law in society, will be in mortal danger. Should we perhaps not, mellowing Cambridge jurisprudence with Cambridge philosophy, qualify Maitland's dictum with Whitehead's axiom that 'the art of progress is to preserve order amid change and to preserve change amid order'?

Our estimate of the place of innovation in the law, and in particular of the legitimacy of judicial innovation, will inevitably be coloured by our fundamental concept of law and our basic estimate of the place of law in world affairs, and these in their turn will depend on our fundamental concept of government and our basic estimate of the need for government, and possibility of government, in a society which transcends the nation state. 'The end of government is the good of mankind.' This pithy maxim is no rhetorical exaggeration of Hegel, Marx, or some latter-day do-gooder, bemused by the omnipresence of the state and proclaiming himself a zealot for collective action. The principle goes back to Aristotle. 'The state came into existence to satisfy the bare needs of life; it continues in existence to make life good.'[1] The maxim itself, as its spare strength suggests, we owe to Locke.[2] We find it reaffirmed by the outstanding veteran of common law scholars, Sir Frederick Pollock. 'Not only material security, but the perfection of human and social life, is what we aim at in that organized co-operation of many men's lives and works which is called the State.'[3] What Aristotle said of the state, and Locke unconsciously broadened to encompass the whole art of government, now applies to 'that organized co-operation of many men's lives and works which is called' the United Nations. Our bailiwick is the whole life of man. The law of nations must reflect the breadth of outlook, depth of insight, and range of foresight implicit in so formidable a responsibility.

A vigorous polity requires a vigorous law. A dynamic polity requires a dynamic law. A responsible polity requires a responsible law. We cannot achieve the ideals of the United Nations or fulfil the obligations of the Charter with a legal philosophy set in any lesser key.

This is not stale stuff. It involves the whole of human destiny. What is the place of law in human destiny as we approach the twenty-first century? Will the inadequacies of the law and a decaying morality surrender large provinces of human conduct to politics, economics, and sociology, and if so with what consequences? What part can the common-law tradition still play in maintaining, where need be reaffirming, and hopefully expanding, the place of law in human destiny? Where are the Mansfield and Marshall of international adjudication?

This is no time for the common law to beat the retreat. The greatest chapter in the expansion of the common law could still lie before it. What part will the contribution to the future of international adjudication of the common-law tradition (not overlooking its equitable strand) play in determining the issue?

[1] *Politics*, Bk. I, Chap. 2.

[2] *Of Civil Government*, para. 229.

[3] *The History of the Science of Politics* (Boston, Beacon Paperbacks, 1960), p. 134.

PRINTED IN GREAT BRITAIN
AT THE UNIVERSITY PRESS, OXFORD
BY VIVIAN RIDLER
PRINTER TO THE UNIVERSITY